Caterpillar Diary

David Drew

RIGBY

Contents

I found a caterpillar and decided to study it.

I made notes about the caterpillar whenever it changed.

I expected it to turn into a butterfly, but it turned into something else instead. Can you guess what it was?

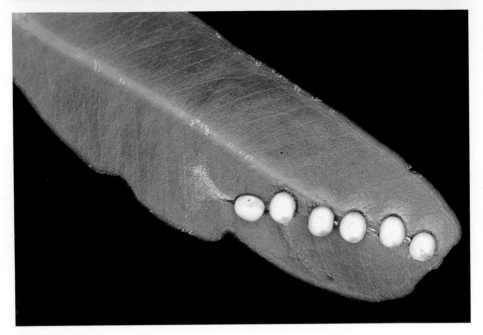

It's the first week of
summer. This morning
I found some tiny eggs
on a leaf.
I decided to
keep them to
see if they hatch.

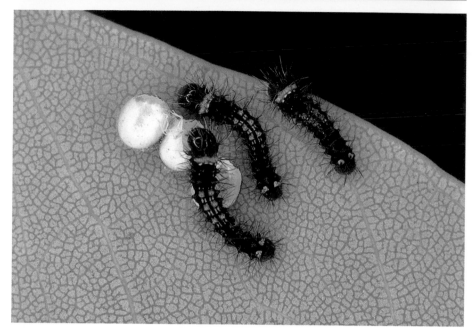

Some of the
caterpillars have
hatched at last.
They're eating
their own
eggshells.

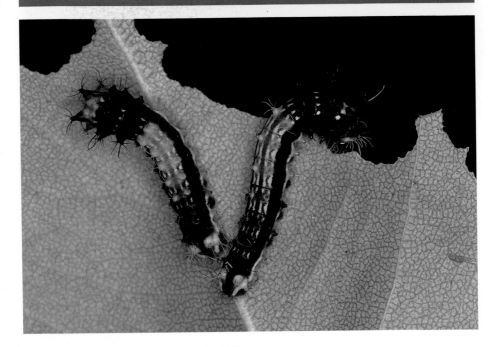

I watched the
caterpillars split
open their skins
and climb out.
I touched one.
The hairs were
prickly.

This caterpillar has shed its skin again. Now it's green and it has grown a lot bigger.

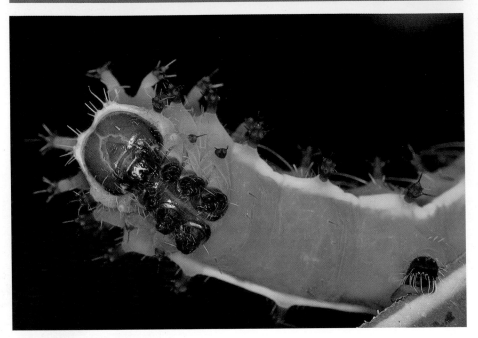

When I use a
magnifying glass
I can see:

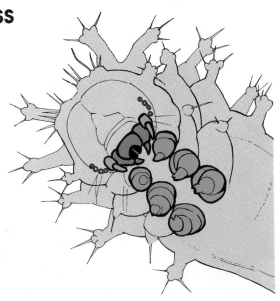

☐ eyes

☐ legs

☐ feelers

☐ mouth

My caterpillar has
changed its
color. This
means it is ready
to become
a pupa.

It has started to
spin a cocoon.
Butterflies don't
make cocoons,
so it's going to
be something
else.

The pupa has been in its cocoon for four weeks now. I can't see any changes. I hope it's all right.

Last night my moth came out of its cocoon. I know it's a moth because its feelers are shaped like feathers.

My moth has two spots on its wings which look like eyes. This scares away birds that might want to eat it.

When I tried to touch the moth it moved its back wings. These have bigger eyespots.

Now I have to let my moth go, so it can feed itself and find a mate.

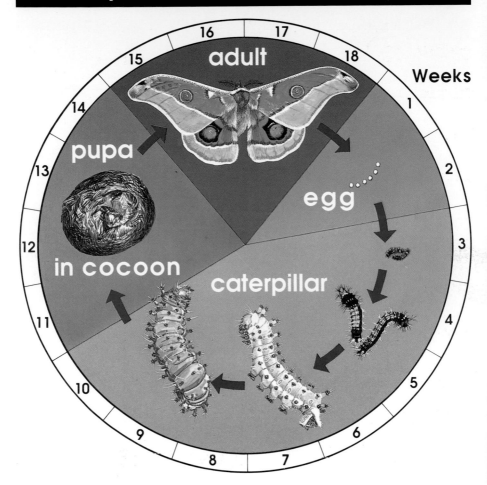

Here is a picture showing my moth's life cycle. It's called an Emperor Gum Moth.

16